The Land of
Whizzing Arrows

by

Simon Chapman

Illustrated by Seb Camagajevac

For Irgen Janco, who guided me through the
Land of Whizzing Arrows

First published in 2007 in Great Britain by
Barrington Stoke Ltd
18 Walker St, Edinburgh EH3 7LP

www.barringtonstoke.co.uk

ISBN: 978-1-84299-468-9

Printed in Great Britain by Bell & Bain Ltd

Contents

South America

Amazon Rainforest

Bolivia

Leo's Journey in Bolivia

Riberalta

Swamps of the River Yata

German man's hut. Indian attack

Crocodile Lake

Parentintin Indians

Intro:

No Way Out

Bolivia, South America, 1921

Leo Parcus couldn't see a way out.

His guide, Alfonso, was dead. There was no food left. His horses had gone. Behind him lay the lake. If he went back there, he would be up against waves as tall as men that seemed to spring up out of nowhere.

It was amazing that so far, he hadn't capsized the canoe that he and Alfonso had carved out of a tree trunk. But Leo knew his luck could not hold out for another crossing. And even if it did, there were the crocodiles on the other side. So he would have to stay on the shore.

But which way to go? In the tall grass of the pampa (grasslands), all directions looked the same. The land was pancake flat with no landmarks to aim for. With no horses or mules to carry water, he would be sick from thirst and heat stroke in a matter of hours.

Maybe a rattle-snake would finish him. Maybe a jaguar. Leo could picture ants running over his body as he lay there, helpless, with vultures flying in to peck at his flesh.

But he could not stay where he was by the lake. Twice now, Indians had shot arrows at him. He knew that he would not be so lucky as to escape a third attack.

Think! Leo knew he had to focus his mind on getting out. He had to squeeze out his fear to stop his mind from shutting off. He could so easily break down and cry, and he knew that if he started sobbing, he just wouldn't stop. Then it might as well be over. Whether it was hunger, thirst, a rattle-snake or Indian arrows – it was all the same in the end. He had seen men break down like that during the First World War. Leo had been an officer in the German army. He knew that when shells were exploding all around you, you had to keep your head clear. Sitting still and doing nothing would get you killed. There was always a way out.

He just could not think of it right now.

Chapter 1
Gateway to the Wilderness

Four Months Earlier . . .

Leo Parcus had arrived in Bolivia in 1920, two years after the First World War had ended. The idea of settling down in Munich in Germany, where he had grown up, did not interest him any more. He wanted to go to a place where his survival would be down to *him* and the choices *he* made. He would to go to the Amazon to explore the wilderness. He would meet – and stay with – the Indians of the rainforest, and find out what it was like to truly live.

He ended up in the jungle town of Riberalta, a collection of wooden huts on the banks of a giant, muddy river. There were a few other people from Europe there, making money from selling rubber, which was made from the sap of trees that grow deep in the forest. Not that these men collected the latex sap. They just used Indians to do the work. And they paid the Indians almost nothing for doing it. Leo thought it was slave labour. But he knew the town would be the best place to find someone who would be his guide and to buy the things he needed to set off on his adventure.

He had heard of a lake in the pampa grassland called Lake Rocaquardo, which was so far away from any towns that it hadn't been put on the maps yet. In the past there had been tribes of Indians who lived around the lake. Hundreds of years ago these tribes had fought off attacks from the people of the powerful Inca empire of the Andes Mountains. And later, these tribes had defended themselves against the Spanish who came to look for gold.

No one had been there and returned to tell the tale. People from the town said that a tribe called the Parentintin lived there now. The stories said they killed anyone who entered their territory. Perhaps they were cannibals. In the pampa grassland, they said, if you weren't a Parentintin, then you were food.

But Leo wasn't going to believe every story he heard. A blank patch of map; the chance of meeting unknown tribes. To Leo, this was like an invitation. He knew he had to go.

Chapter 2
Swamp Forest!

For Leo, finding Alfonso was a fantastic stroke of luck. When Leo said they would be going to visit 'wild savages', Alfonso said, "No problem." The trip would take months. "No problem." They might end up getting eaten. Again, "No problem." Maybe this scruffy looking Indian (who turned up wearing just a pair of trousers and carrying only a bow and arrow) didn't understand what Leo was talking about, or maybe he was trying to get away from someone. Certainly, he seemed very pleased to be leaving town and grateful for the money, the shirts – and the gun – that Leo gave him.

They set off shortly after the end of the wet season. Leo had bought a white horse, which he named Amigo ('friend') and two huge hounds, trained to hunt jaguars, called Togo and Tigre. Alfonso had a brown mule to ride. Another mule (white, and very stubborn) followed up behind with all of the luggage.

It should have been easy crossing the grassland, as the ground was flat and open. But the white mule felt hard done by with its load of food, boxes of bullets and small gifts for the 'wild savages'. Every few hundred metres the mule would roll on its back and try to get rid of its load. When they reached an area of forest, their progress got even slower.

Leo set to work, hacking a path through the undergrowth with his long, sharp machete (bush knife). It was hot, sweaty work and soon he was wishing that he had brought more water to drink. Leo was annoyed that he had to cut his trail extra wide so that the horses could get through.

He pushed his way forward, clearing small trees that got in the way and slicing the vines which kept looping over the horses' necks. It was hard enough work on level ground, but when the land was rough or water-logged, it became a nightmare.

The first hour wasn't too bad, but then the ground got swampy. The mules kept sinking up to their bellies in water, mud

and slime. Leo and Alfonso pulled, whipped and yelled at them until they moved. The insects were terrible. Clouds of mosquitoes and tiny black marahui flies swarmed around the horses' heads, driving them insane.

Suddenly, eyes staring as if with madness, the white horse called Amigo charged forward – and sank. With almost super-human effort, Leo kept the animal's head above water. He pulled Amigo up onto drier land. But there were more problems to come. A fallen tree trunk, 200 feet long, blocked their way. The trunk was too high to get over and getting around was nearly as difficult. When the tree had tumbled it had brought down all its neighbours and now, between the broken mass of branches and trunks, tangles of vines had grown up. Leo and Alfonso hacked forward with their machetes, but it was painfully slow going.

The ground in the forest now went from being just marshy to totally flooded. To their surprise this made the going easier – for a while – as Leo and Alfonso could lead the two mules and the horse between the trees with nothing getting in the way.

Leo could not see where he was putting his feet as the water was so murky. He had to feel his way forward and hope there was nothing in the way that might trip him up. He tried not to think about what might be swimming around next to his legs. Electric eels that could knock him senseless with a 600 volt shock. Sting rays with poisonous tail spines that would stab into his leg if he stepped on one. There would be flesh-eating piranhas. Leo knew that the fish didn't normally bite unless you were bleeding. But that didn't stop him worrying every time something brushed past his leg.

He knew he had to stop thinking like this. He had to focus his mind. The way forward was open and he could lead the horses easily. His progress was good. Perhaps too good. He and his horse Amigo were now well out in front with Alfonso far behind with the mules. Then Leo stepped forward ...

And sank.

Chapter 3

Through the Swamps

Under the water Leo was in full panic. He had taken in a lungful of water. Acting on instinct he tried desperately to reach the surface. But his foot was stuck. Thrashing around was pointless. He would die soon if he didn't get a grip. His knife! – Yes, he still had it. It was in his hand. He had to reach down and cut.

He felt around for the root that held him and he sawed with the blade. Back and forth. Then he pulled as hard as he could. At last he was free, his head out of the water. He could breathe again. Propping himself up on the horse he gulped air until he felt calm again.

A group of howler monkeys, disturbed by the noise, crashed away through the treetops. Parrots shrieked above him. Two pink spoonbills flew up, clattering into the air and gliding away over the lake that stretched out in front of Leo and Alfonso.

It was clear they would have to swim it. But it would be like swimming through soup. Clouds of marahui flies and mosquitoes buzzed around their heads. Tabano flies stung them with bites that punched into their skin like a stapler. The mules, even the stubborn white one, swam the lake happily enough. But for Amigo the horse, it was another matter. Speckled with blood spots and worn out, he was at his limit.

He made it across, but when he saw more swamps and bushes on the other side, he lay down as if to say, "I give up." Leo almost decided to shoot him to end his suffering, but then he saw they were close to a river. Maybe things would get better ahead.

The misery of the swamps lasted three more days. Weak from crossing the lake, Amigo was nearly washed away in the river. The brown mule lost its load – the tea, the sugar and all of the salt – in a stream. But the ground began to dry out, and then, suddenly, the swamp forest ended. The open pampa grassland stretched out once more before them, and the spirits of the two men lifted.

Chapter 4
Alfonso's Tall Stories

Four days later, the pair reached a ranch. This was really nothing more than a one-roomed wooden house that was home to a few Indians from the Chacobo tribe. There were also some cowboys. Their job was to look after the herds of white cattle that ran wild in the grassland.

Only one or two boats came up the nearby river in a year to bring supplies and take cows away to market, so Leo and Alfonso's arrival was a big event. The explorers were treated like heroes – and Alfonso was set on playing the part. He told the cowboys all about the swamps and how in the pampa he had found two jaguar cubs and given them to Leo. Leo had been chased by the angry mother until he had thrown the cubs down. This, the truth, was fantastic enough, but Alfonso added more. He had Leo grabbing a jaguar cub out of its mother's jaws and then slitting her throat with his machete.

"Do you really think they believed you?" Leo asked him afterwards.

All Alfonso could reply was, "Does it matter if some of it was untrue? They enjoyed it and that's what counts."

"And", Alfonso added, "it gave you time to ask about where we go next."

"To Lake Rocaquardo," Leo said, pointing south. "They say there's another German man who lives there. He is alone apart from his pack of dogs that protect him from the Indians who are always trying to kill him. The cowboys have never travelled as far as the lake. They say it's too dangerous. They call it 'The Land of Whizzing Arrows'."

Chapter 5

The Land of Whizzing Arrows

Two days later. Riding through the pampa grassland again.

The still air filled with a rumble that felt like an earthquake as 300 or 400 cows rushed out of the head-high grass, running past Leo and Alfonso. What had set them off? There could be Indians close by, but the two hunting dogs, Togo and Tigre, hadn't picked up any scent. It must be a false alarm. The two men rode on.

A flock of black ducks flew up and swept over their heads.

Suddenly, Alfonso grabbed the back of Leo's head and pushed it down onto his horse's neck. Several arrows swooshed past.

"Gallop!" Alfonso yelled.

When they had made what they judged to be a safe distance, Alfonso and Leo stopped.

"The cattle spooked me," Alfonso said. "Then when the ducks flew up, I knew that there must be Indians here. Then I saw the top of a bow sticking up. The Indians were less than a spear's throw behind us."

They reached the German man's house by the lake after 11 hours of riding. Leo couldn't wait to meet him. He hadn't spoken his own language for months and was looking forward to talking about Germany.

But the house turned out to be empty. Inside, there were several Indian arrows propped against one of the walls. There was a bed made up of a jaguar skin thrown over a pile of dried grass. Leo decided that he and Alfonso would stay there for a couple of days in the hope that the German man would return.

The nearest place to wash and fetch water was some way away. Because of the danger of Indian attack, Leo and Alfonso went together. On the second afternoon they found a red feather flight from an arrow. It had not been there in the morning. Was this some sort of warning?

The two hurried back to the hut. They did not go out there for water again.

Leo did not sleep well that night. He had nightmares about how he and Alfonso would escape without being shot by arrows. Then Alfonso shook him awake.

"The Indians are outside, not far off. We must get to the horses now or we'll lose them."

Leo and Alfonso crept outside and advanced into the long grass on all fours. And waited. Togo and Tigre's ears pricked up. Was there movement in the reeds ahead? Leo hardly dared breathe for fear that any sound would give away their position.

"Get down!"

Leo hit the ground at the same moment as Alfonso fired his rifle, and a volley of arrows sped past their heads. Leo shot into the reeds, and let the hunting dogs loose.

"Fetch them!"

Alfonso fired again. There was a scream, and Leo was running forward, gun in hand.

He made fifteen strides. There, lying in a patch of flattened grass, bleeding from bites to the arm and neck, was the dead body of an Indian hunter.

Leo was nearly sick with fear. He could hear his heart pounding. He could feel his skin go cold and clammy with shock. His dogs had done their job too well. They had killed a man and the other Indians would be out for revenge. Leo and Alfonso had to leave right now.

Chapter 6
The Lake of Despair

For the first day after the killing, Leo and Alfonso rode without stopping. On horseback in the pampa grassland they knew they could outrun any Indians on foot. Also, they hoped that in this open country they would be able to see any Indians before they came close enough to fire their arrows. Only one thing caused them to slow down that first day. Dogs.

They knew the pack of dogs had to belong to the German whose house they had been using for the last two nights. For a moment Leo was glad that he would meet him at last. But the dogs were running right at them – an attack course. Togo and Tigre ran out to stop them and Alfonso fired off several shots to scare them away. "Those dogs," he said, "are running wild. I think their owner must be dead."

Time seemed to lose meaning as the two men fled the lake and carried on southwards. They met and killed another jaguar. Their feet were covered with maggot-filled boils where sand-fleas had dug into their skin after the men had walked barefoot by a dried-up stream.

One day, a wild bull stood in their path and, when they shot it, a second bull came thundering out of the bushes straight towards them. Alfonso dived off the brown mule and shot at the bull at exactly the same time as Leo fired. Both bullets hit. The bull fell, then got up and charged at Alfonso, who fumbled with his rifle – and missed. For a split second it looked like the end for Alfonso. But Leo's second shot found its mark. The bull went down – right on top of Alfonso. Luckily, he was all right. He pulled himself out from under the dead bull, without a scratch.

The pair carried on riding south. Finally, after two weeks or so they reached a second lake, and they stopped. They couldn't face days of trekking around it so they decided to set their animals loose, build a canoe, and travel across the water.

Building the boat took just two days, an incredible feat considering they only had machetes to bring down a tree trunk and carve it into shape. They used fire to eat into the wood in the middle so that they could hollow out the log.

The dugout canoe they ended up with floated, but it rocked about a lot and felt really unsafe. This shouldn't have been a problem on flat lake waters, but away from the shore they found the water was far from flat. Waves rose up suddenly, crashing over the boat and almost capsizing it. Leo thought there might be an earthquake under the lake. Soon Leo and Alfonso were desperate to reach dry land.

But, once more, there was a catch. The lake was full of caimans (South American crocodiles), some as long as eight metres. Hundreds of them.

To make matters worse Leo couldn't even get to the shore. The canoe grounded with fifteen metres to go. It would not budge. Now they could move neither forwards nor back. To shift the boat or walk to shore would mean getting into the water. And, with crocodiles all around them, neither Leo nor Alfonso was going to try that.

Chapter 7
Crocodile Attack

How many times must Leo have replayed in his memory what happened next? How many times must he have gone through every move, every decision? But you can't re-run what has already passed. What had happened, had happened, and Leo had to live with it.

There was a tree with a low branch that hung over the water. Leo thought he could get to it before the crocodiles got to him.

He ran the length of the boat and jumped as far as he could. Then he waded the few steps until he could reach the branch and pulled himself out of the water. He was safe.

It was Alfonso's turn next. But the crocodiles that had been log-still moments before had now sensed the movement. With barely a ripple of their tails, several were gliding towards the canoe. More of a worry was that some had sunk from view.

Alfonso repeated Leo's move. He sprinted along the boat, leaped, and – *Snap*!

Just out of grabbing distance of Leo and the branch, Alfonso went down. Leo watched, unable to help, as his friend kicked out and broke free of the crocodile's bite. His leg half off, Alfonso threw himself forwards as Leo reached out his hand.

"Hold on!" yelled Leo, trying to pull out his belt so that he could loop it over his friend.

"Leo, Leo," Alfonso gasped. Then he was pulled down again into the water as a crocodile bit his left arm off.

Leo heard the crunch as another reptile's mouth closed on his friend's chest. He fired his pistol into the croc's skull, killing it. But it was no use. The water was red now. A heaving mass of crocodiles were pulling at the one Leo had shot and at what remained of Alfonso.

Leo knew he must not let himself be frozen by fear into doing nothing. He had to get back to the boat, which was floating now there was no one in it to keep it down. But he could not reach it. And he could not go into the water to get to it.

Working fast, he cut his leather belt into long, thin strips. He knotted the pieces together and tied a forked stick at one end. Then, lying on the branch, he swung his homemade fishing line at the canoe until the stick hook caught on it. Now he could pull the boat closer to him. There were crocodiles along each side. His next move was critical.

He dropped into the canoe. It nearly rolled over but somehow Leo kept his balance. He was afloat again.

Staying close to the palm trees by the water's edge, Leo looked round for a crocodile-free place to land the canoe. He was still half-crazed with fear since his friend's awful death. He went round a headland and saw that the shore was curving away from him. Another chilling truth hit him. This was not the other side of the lake, as he had supposed. This was an island.

It was an awful moment. He could stay here and die slowly from hunger or he could paddle through crocodile-infested waters and huge waves back to where he had started.

For three days, he lost his mind. He let despair wash over him and he was sure that he would die whatever he did. But, in the end he pulled through. He pushed the boat off into the lake and started paddling back.

Chapter 8
Surrender

So now we are back where the story started. Leo had made it back across the lake and reached the open pampa once more. Now, with his back to the water, Leo Parcus made the decision to live.

To his surprise, it wasn't hard to find Amigo and the two mules. There was lots of fresh green grass by the lake's edge and

the animals had stayed close by. His
hunting dogs, Togo and Tigre also hadn't
wandered far, so Leo soon found them too.
Then he found the saddles, the guns and a
few spare supplies from where he had
hidden them. He loaded up the horses and
set off across the grassland. He rode south
as before. He thought he would either come
to a village or meet Indians.

Over the days riding south he had
narrow escapes from wild bulls and a herd
of peccaries (like pigs) that charged him
when he shot two of their number for food.
Water and good grass for the horses to eat
were becoming difficult to find. The pampa
was oven-hot for much of the day, and
every stream he found was dried up. He
had to dig into the dried mud at the bottom
just to get a sip of filthy water. He knew
that soon they would not be able to carry on.

When he saw the glow of a fire in the distance his spirits lifted. Even though he was sure it was an Indian campfire, he decided he would go towards it. He would surrender himself to the Indians. They would either kill him or give him water, he reckoned. Either way had to be better than dying of thirst.

He crept closer. A crowd of tribesmen and women were sitting around a fire talking softly. They wore no clothes. Some had yellow and red feather head-dresses. Leo knew they were from the Parentintin tribe – the ones he knew were man-eaters – and that they hadn't spotted him yet. He didn't want to appear a threat to them so, without making a sound, he put his gun on the floor and took off all of his clothes. Then, stark naked, he walked into the circle of firelight.

Chapter 9
Contact

The jungle Indians do not think in the same way as people brought up in cities, who are used to cars, trains and houses made of stone. Leo didn't know what the Parentintin tribe would do when he walked naked into their camp. He half expected to be shot through with arrows. He wasn't expecting silence. He could feel every eye trained on him. No one moved. The stillness seemed to drag on forever.

Suddenly ...

"Hiiiiiaaahahahuhuhuaaaaa!"

One of the men shouted.

"Hihahahu!" Leo screamed back the first thing that came into his head.

"How," the tribesman shouted.

An old woman pushed a water container towards Leo's mouth. He took a sip, and then drained it to the bottom.

"Hau," said the Indian and gave him more drink.

After a while all the Indians got up and started walking off. Leo ran back to where he had left his clothes, got dressed and gathered up his animals. He got up onto his horse and followed the line of people as they walked through the night to a huge wood and palm-leaf house in a clearing in the forest.

After that first meeting, the Parentintin tribe took no notice of Leo. He set up a camp on the other side of the clearing, across from the strange house. He watched the villagers' pet monkeys, coatis (animals like raccoons) and parrots. He kept out of the way of the tame jaguars. The Indians didn't talk to him. They did not seem interested in him. They weren't bothered when he took his horses out of the forest and into the grassland to graze. He could have escaped. But was he a prisoner? Leo just didn't know.

Leo decided he must make the first step and try to speak with the people of the Parentintin tribe. The man who had first shouted at him seemed to be the chief. Leo gave him one of his shirts. He tried playing with some of the children but they were scared of him.

The only members of the village that paid him any attention were a tame peccary pig that followed him around like a little dog, an old woman, and a girl who snuggled up with him one night while he was sleeping in the longhouse. Leo tried to ask the chief who she was. He acted it out but he couldn't tell if he had made himself understood. The chief grinned and pushed the girl into his arms. The girl's name was Shiggi Shiggi. Leo, it seemed, now had a wife!

Chapter 10
The Arrow-shot Body

Leo relaxed. He now felt part of the village. He went with Shiggi Shiggi to the pampa to exercise the horses. He feasted and went on hunting trips with the tribe. He began to have a deep respect for the way the Parentintin lived in harmony with nature. He showed the Indians how to ride a horse and how to throw a rope lasso. And he gave away more of his clothes and belongings. Shiggi Shiggi made him a chief's head-dress – out of parrot feathers. Leo felt quite content ... until the day a dead body was brought into the village.

Looking at the feathers he wore, Leo worked out that the man was from a different tribe. Three broken-off arrows stuck out of his chest. The village was full of excitement. The seven men who had carried the body were shouting. So were the women and children who had come to join in. The hunters threw the dead man to the ground and a few women grabbed the body and started dragging it towards the house.

Leo moved forward for a better look. What were they doing? Were they showing their respect for the dead man? No! Leo was nearly sick at what he saw next.

The women got out their bamboo knives and cut off the man's hands and feet. Then

they dragged the body to the nearby trees
where it was set upon by the village's
peccary pigs. The chief picked up the cut-
off hands and feet and, to the whoops and
cheers of the rest of the tribe, took them to
the fire to cook. Leo at last knew what it
all meant.

The Parentintin were man-eaters.

Chapter 11
Escape

After seeing the man's body hacked to pieces, Leo knew he had to escape. But he had a problem. He was now so much part of the village that he couldn't just gather up his stuff and go. So he went about his daily life but all the time he was secretly getting together everything that he needed for the trek he and Shiggi Shiggi would make.

That way, when the time came for them to leave they would be ready.

He went hunting again with the Parentintin. This time the target wasn't a spider monkey or a peccary pig. It was a man. Leo was one of the first to see him. He was desperate to warn the man off. But that would risk his own life, so he kept silent.

Like the other victim, the Indian was from the Chacobo tribe. The Parentintin hunters shot him with six arrows and carried his body joyfully back to their village. The chief presented Leo with the dead man's bow and arrows out of respect, as he was one of the heroes of the hunt. But Leo felt awkward. He tried to push the gifts back into the chief's hands but the chief would not take them.

Leo sat at the edge of the camp that night, keeping well out of the way when the cooked body parts of the dead Chacobo Indian were passed around the hunters of the tribe. Leo did not eat with them.

The feasting that followed would have been a perfect chance for Leo to leave the village without being seen. But he did not. He wanted to teach Shiggi Shiggi how to ride so that the two of them could escape together on horseback. Before Leo had arrived, the girl had never seen horses.

It took some time to over-come her fear for the animals but once that was done, she soon became a skilled rider. She never really worked out how to use the reins to steer the mule. Whenever she wanted it to turn, she would spit at one of its ears!

Leo and Shiggi Shiggi made their break for freedom the next time the village had a feast. Leo waited until most of the Indians were drunk on corn beer and starting to fall asleep. Then he went to find his 'wife'. He was pleased that she wanted to come with him. He knew it was an important choice for her to make. Once she left the tribe she would never be allowed to return.

The pair led the horses and dogs out to the place in the pampa where Leo had hidden his gear. They saddled up and set off into the night.

Chapter 12
On the Run!

Leo allowed them to slow down after three days. By then he thought that they must be far ahead of any Parentintin hunters following on foot. Shiggi Shiggi, riding the brown mule, suffered in the heat, and Leo was glad when the first rains of the wet season began to fall. Now at least it would be cooler and finding drinking water would no longer be a problem.

The pair made their way slowly forward for many weeks. Leo and Shiggi Shiggi came across anacondas and tapirs (Leo was pulled off his horse when he tried to lasso one with a rope). They were getting closer to town. There were fences across the grassland, more cattle, and ranches where the cowboys stared, amazed to see an Indian girl riding a mule.

At last, Leo and Shiggi Shiggi reached the town of Riberalta. They were back where Leo had started out 8 months before. They went up to the house of a man Leo had met before. He too was German. But when he saw them he got out his shot-gun. He couldn't work out who this wild-haired man was, wearing an Indian tree-bark shirt, with a man-eating Parentintin woman riding beside him. It was only when the man heard Leo call to him in German that he worked out who he was, Leo Parcus was alive!

And what happened next?

Leo Parcus went back to Germany. He lost his bow and arrows in a train crash in France on the way home, but he did manage to rescue the chief's head-dress that Shiggi Shiggi had made him.

Shiggi Shiggi remained in the town of Riberalta at the German man's house where she looked after his collection of jungle animals.

The Parentintin Indians have almost all died out. There are still a few living in Brazil.

The Chacobo Indians still live in small groups, hunting peccary pigs and deer in the forest and pampa grassland of North Bolivia.

Barrington Stoke would like to thank all its readers for commenting on the manuscript before publication and in particular:

Danielle Chalmers
Chloe Copland
David Craig
Robbie Gatherer
Reece Harris
Christopher Jenks
Lauren Kennedy
Peter Mansfield
Kirsty McAllister
Conner McBride
Kalvin McCabe
Chloe McCluskie

David McIntyre
Luisaidh McMaster
Jordan McMenamin
Mrs L. McMurray
Daniel Morgan
Rachael Mulholland
Emma-Louise Orr
David Pirie
Ryan Regan
Mrs L. Shedden
Kerry Travers
Melanie J. West

Become a Consultant!

Would you like to give us feedback on our titles before they are published? Contact us at the e-mail address below – we'd love to hear from you!

info@barringtonstoke.co.uk
www.barringtonstoke.co.uk

Simon's Diary:

To Bolivia and beyond!

In 2005 Simon Chapman set off to follow in the foot-steps of Leo Parcus ... turn the page for a secret look at his real life jungle diary!

My left arm is really painful with blisters that look and feel like burns. There were stinging bees all around us.

Croc count
Today's score:
Lagato (spectacled caiman) - 100 +
Capybara - around 40
Black caiman - 20 - 30
1 dolphin
+ 1 dead anteater floating in the river

Snake birds poke their dagger beaks out of the water and red-eyed hoatzins that look like something out of the Jurassic era hiss and cough as we go past. Capybaras, like sheep-sized guinea pigs, duck under the water - and more worryingly, crocodiles slide into the water as we pass.

a capybara

While I've been writing this, we've pulled up next to a dead crocodile - 2 and 1/2 meters long. Its jaws could crush a cow's skull. This, Irgen our guide says, is only half grown. No one wants to wash or swim.

Anaconda. 2 metres long.

I feel a bit bad as it bit Billy quite nastily on the hand while he was holding it for me to draw.

We saw what we thought was a capybara crossing to the right. I looked through my binoculars and followed it. Then we saw what it really was ... a jaguar!

Jaguar tracks

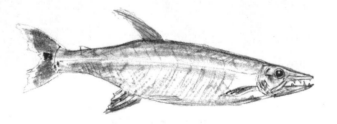

This jumped into the boat

I really think the man who met us at the ranch had cat's eyes - pupils like slits. He oozed power.

******

At times it's enormous fun. Yesterday, just before sunset we spotted a shaggy red-maned wolf and followed it across the pampa - wow!

Horses sweat.
They don't show you that in cowboy films.

We knew that if we capsized we would lose everything
we owned ... and possibly meet the caimans ...

Stingrays hide themselves on the river bed and if
you tread on them flick up their spiked tails. These
can give you a painful gash!